Wet Dreams

and Placid Silence

Scott Shaw

Buddha Rose Publications

10 9 8 7 6 5 4 3 2 1
Printed in the United States of America

WET DREAMS

AND PLACID SILENCE

1

I saw her somewhere
a long time ago
somewhere

somewhere
     in a distant daydream
somewhere lost in a fantasy
a long way off
somewhere
     on a tranquil highway
stretching off into infinity

somewhere

somewhere
     in last night's dream
and today's fantasy

sitting staring out of
      bamboo shades
bamboo shades
lead out to a summer's day
bamboo shades/prison bars
life in the big city

watching a movie on t.v.
isolation
the unity of isolation
easy unity
passive submission
a saved life
in an elementary vision

easy to save
a saved life

moments
in the life
of an unwilling recluse

3

it was almost a fragment
in a far off dream
naked in the window

I stand
eyes gazing at her

"where do you want to go;
heaven?"
"can people have sex
in heaven?"
"I don't know.
why don't you ask God."
"no, I think heaven is only
for people who say
that they don't
think about sex."

5

they sat on the grass
overlooking the park
he poured the wine
and handed her a glass
she asked,
"do you love me?"
he said,
"I'd love to love you
but I don't think it will happen.
so, I will settle for
momentary infatuation."
they both smiled
he extended his glass
and said,
"to us and the moment."
the glasses touched

french photo magazine
cover girl
oh...
too beautiful

inside
one of those
perfectly designed
full haired pussys
ah...
too much lust

indonesian beauty on the cover
french full haired pussy
on the inside
too much
too much lust
I must put
this magazine away

7

one girl sitting
in a group of male japanese
I catch her stare
just for a moment
is her fantasy
similar to mine?

8

I wish I had a shower
that stayed warm all night
I would sit and relax
let the water
run over me
like in my younger days

I sit back tonight
in the fleeting hot water
and space out
into casual ecstasy
casual insanity
I just let it happen

no one
to be bohemian with
left to my own devise
left to my own demise
I sit
in a quickly cooling shower
and space out
into casual ecstasy
casual insanity
and I just let it happen

9

out with another korean girl
she plays hard to get
she wants it
I want it
but she plays hard to get

> I never met a woman
> who played hard to get

her body
not so bad
my arm around her
I feel a little fat
that's OK though

I look into her eyes
her face
casual asian beauty

I fall in love
well, I always fall in love
I am seeking
broken heart feeling(s)
but any feeling(s) will do

feelings
love
something
anything
only a moment
that's all it lasts for

I take her to my place
apartment on the beach
how quickly her
hard to get
fades
she falls into my arms
I remove her clothing
we do what we do what we do
done and over
god, I am already so bored
with her

10

love is cheap
find any woman
age 23+
not yet married
or formerly married
and they tell you
that they understand you
that they will change for you
that they will do anything
for you
and all the other bullshit

love is cheap
love is easy
just a promise
just a lie
say, yes

love is cheap

top ramen
and a heineken
for dinner
tripping over
musical instruments
and travel stuff
upon the floor

I never seem to unpack
until I am ready to be back
on the road

me, all alone again
artist?

12

it is funny
how times change
and what I now love...

it is funny
how good feelings
sometimes they come from
nowhere

romance
enlightenment
happiness
all alone
to sit down
and drink coffee

I sit here
the t.v. is on
        star trek
reading a magazine
guitar beside me
pack of peanut m and m's
in front of me
drinking coffee

enlightenment comes
in strange forms

13

well, I went out
had some
outdoor
in the rain
ah...
cafe mocha
and chocolate moose
alone

the lady who works there
the one I went to see
she was not there
so, I came alone
left alone
only the paradise
of the moment
in the nighttime rain
to occupy my time

I went to my p.o. box
checked it
nada
I came home

no worthy messages
placed upon
my telephone
answering machine
so, what to do?
all alone
come home
into creative aloneness
feel the moment
trip over the instruments
on the floor
on the coach
on the walls
and maybe
just maybe
I'll go out
and take a walk
in the rain

14

well, I think
that I could probably
do without the hamburger
for it is after 2:00 am
but do with out the illusion
no, I do not think so
for she was looking good
and my mind is roaming
so I'll have to go down
and see that
sweet little latin girl
who finally smiled at me
last night
down there
at the 24 hours a day
hamburger joint

15

plotting mind
lies
into her body
the lies
I have told
I continue to tell
the desire
it is the same
strong
one purpose
one pointed
one goal
an obtainable goal
obtainable
only through lies
lies
that keep me in
the arms of various women

16

I see you
through the window
last week
I saw you
open
the closing door
this week
will I know you
will I hold you

see the colors
of make-up fade
as they run from her face
in the cool winter rain

18

tonight I hear you
divine mother ocean waves
I hear you
through my window
I wish
I was closer to you
but then, I wish a lot of things
but for tonight
it is nice
to hear you
through my living room
window

yes, I would like
to go to venice with you
yes, I would like
to hold your hand

I'd like you to be
what you never were
something more
than just my pretend

20

funny how my life
always seems to be
either too much rush
or too much nothing to do

       too much rush
       filled with fantasies
       for another time

       nothing to do
       filled with fantasies
       for another time

       life...

so, I go to my p.o. box
get rejection notices
I guess it is better
than going there
and having nothing
       waiting at all
but it is hard
to get hit with mindless
rejection

so, friday night
alone
I watch t.v.

21

well, I have made love to
an indonesian girl
a vietnamese girl
so many japanese,
korean,
chinese girls
that I long ago lost count

asian being my preference
white/black
and all those in between
hold little importance
at least in regards
to this poem

now I would love
to love them
love them
all again
but you know
that I know
that you can never go back

I thought to fall in love
with a chinese fantasy
as I returned from
my last journey

but
as it turns out
she is a mere
           seventeen years of age
so, I smiling must step back
back for a year or so...

           the age
           not so much a problem
           but the situation
           that is what will get you

on the outside
is the outside
the far side of this dream

I think back
a few years deep
there was this filipina
of a babe

but my interest in her
was lost
lost before it ever began
      she promised me
      everything
      I took nothing

so me
I am sitting here
sitting on a friday night
listening to the
      shattering silence
listening to
      the memories
      of my mind

I would love to have someone
to hold onto tonight
someone's shoulder
to lay down upon
      for as this day
      has continued
      I have become
      more and more depressed
      but I don't get depressed
      about being depressed

I have asked this question
so many times
why must I be so alone
where can I go
to dance
where can I go
to fall in love
with more than
momentary women
      worthless fantasies

but
tomorrow
it is another day
a new time
a new time to start
a new life
to start in

tomorrow
that is a good place to start

     square one

22

some how
some way
if I change the channel
on the television set
in just the right way
in the right direction
I will go back in time
I will find myself
in Burma
and in the arms
of my forever
true love

waves of heat
in the distance
asian chance
between them and I
I look for the eyes of romance
I look deeply into them
but they have nothing to say
so I get up
turn
and I walk away

www.ingramcontent.com/pod-product-compliance
Lightning Source LLC
Chambersburg PA
CBHW060810110426
42739CB00032BA/3167